6.10.2015

My Darling
Sister Brenda
Lots of love
Pat
xxx

Brenda Buckingham

BACK TO BLACK

Editor and Writer: Cathy Galvin
Editor and Design: Stephen Reid

Researcher: Stephen Munns
Contributors: Sophie Haydock, Mel Bradman

First published in the United Kingdom in 2013 by:
Evans Mitchell Books
5th Floor
130 City Road
London
EC1V 2NW
United Kingdom
www.embooks.co.uk
Copyright © 2013 Evans Mitchell Books

British Library Cataloguing in Publication Data
A CIP record of this book is available on request
from the British Library.

ISBN: 978-1-901268-64-5

Printed in the UK by Butler Tanner & Dennis Ltd

Evans Mitchell Books

THE STORY OF CILLA

Anyone who had a heart would be moved by the story of Britain's top-selling female recording artist of the Sixties: Cilla Black. By the age of 21 she had jumped from obscurity as a clerk-typist in Liverpool to chart success.

Warm, glamorous, mischievous: this volume captures the confidence, egalitarianism and vivacity of a performer who personified the heady freedom of her time. It also celebrates her 50 unique years in showbusiness — conquering that formative decade in the charts, on television and with top billing in the West End; going on to become Britain's most loved television presenter with the audience-busting shows Surprise! Surprise! and Blind Date. She's still surprising us today.

Her story is a magical blend of grit and grace. The only woman managed by Brian Epstein, the genius behind the Mersey sound and the success of her friends, The Beatles, she was described by him in this way: "She is what she is — an untutored girl from a happy working-class family in a lowly part of Liverpool. She's not easily intimidated by anything or anyone." He spotted the artistry in those qualities.

The photographs in this book celebrate that unique talent and life.

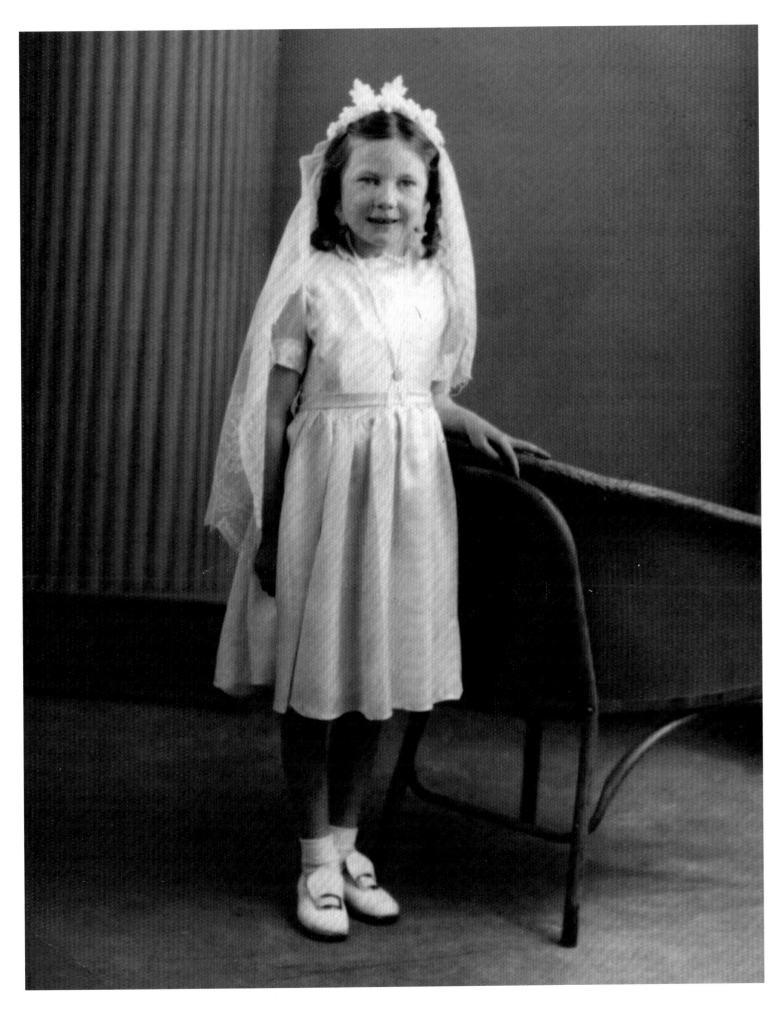

Above and left: Cilla today. Previous page: her first communion, aged 7

FROM THE TYPING POOL TO TOP OF THE CHARTS

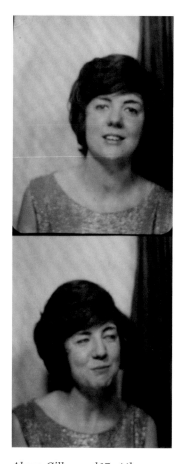

Above: Cilla, aged 17, at the Zodiac club — where she would later meet her husband, Bobby, in the early 1960s. Opposite: the flat above the barber's shop on Scotland Road, where she grew up

I was waiting for the call that would change my life. I'd been standing in the phone box for two hours, praying that my manager Brian Epstein would ring at midday. It was a freezing February Sunday in Liverpool near me Mam and Dad's flat on Scottie: Scotland Road. I was so excited I only moved when someone knocked on the window and told me to get out because they had to make a call. Thank God nobody had to ring 999 that morning because I'd have fought anyone off. Brian was ringing from London to let me know how my single, Anyone Who Had A Heart, was doing in the charts. I was watching the minutes, and when he didn't call on time, I began to panic, assuming it was bad news, knowing he was quite shy and suspecting he didn't know how to tell me. My first single had got to No 35 the year before, and it was quite possible I'd be a one-hit wonder.

Then the call came. He told me: "It's selling nearly 100,000 copies a day. It's at No 1."

I ran out of the phone box beside myself with happiness, but who could I share it with? This was 1964 and nobody I knew had their own phone. Mam was working on her secondhand clothing stall at the market; Dad was down at the docks; my older brothers George and John were out, and my boyfriend Bobby was working in the bakery at Woolworths, so I celebrated by going to the hairdressers in town because I thought I could afford to splash out. I had my hair recoloured: I'd been dying it red with sevenpenny Camilla-tone rinses and I wanted it done properly. The photographers tracked me down under the dryer, and later in the day the local paper took me down to take pictures in the docks where my dad worked but he hid.

Suddenly, I was famous. Brian had chosen the song for me, written by Burt Bacharach and Hal David, after hearing Dionne Warwick sing it while he was on a trip to New York. The producer George Martin thought it would suit Shirley Bassey better but Brian stuck to his guns and insisted it was for me. A month later, I had my first silver disc for sales in excess of a quarter of a million. In the Top Ten below me were hugely successful bands including The Rolling Stones, Gerry and the Pacemakers and The Tremeloes. That single became the UK's biggest selling single by a female artist in the Sixties.

Five months earlier, my Dad had let Brian become my manager when I was just 20 years old. Quite a few had tried and failed before him. Off the back of the success of The Beatles, we had all these Londoners coming up who had heard me singing round the clubs and thought they could manage me. First, they had to pass the Sunday Teatime Test with my Dad. He had worked in London helping build the Dorchester Hotel and he thought these "cockneys" were all gangsters. Brian was different: at 31, ambitious, quiet and well spoken. My Dad had bought a piano from Brian's father at his furniture shop in Walton Road when I was a child. "The piano's still going strong," he said, "So I may as well sign with his son."

When I first met Brian, I really fancied him. I'd gone in to NEMS, his family's music and electrical store down the road from the Cavern club, the place that would become famous as the centre of Liverpool's music scene. Along with half the females in Liverpool, I wanted a copy of The Beatles singing My Bonnie Lies Over The Ocean on the B-side of a single by another band. Brian realised the band we all wanted to hear must have something about them, and he came to see them perform at The Cavern. He was wearing a navy-blue cashmere coat and a silk-spotted scarf; I thought, he's gorgeous. He was eloquent and lived on Queen's Drive. Very posh! I'd been singing with all the bands since I was 14, and when Brian became interested in working with me, I was working as a clerk-typist at British Insulated Callenders Cables.

My dad nearly changed his mind about signing the contract when he saw what I was going to be called: Cilla Black. The family name was White. It was a miracle I was signed by Brian at all. I'd got to know all The Beatles when my friend Pauline Behan suggested we see her boyfriend playing in a new band at a club called the Iron Door. I was only 15 and studying at Anfield Commercial College. Her boyfriend was George Harrison. At the club, my friends started shouting: "Give Cilla a go!" They wanted the band to

Above: Cilla pays Santa a visit in the early 1950s

let me sing with them. John Lennon said: "Alright, Cyril, let's see what you're made of." I was already great friends with Ringo Starr, then using his own name, Richie Starkey, who at that time was playing with Rory Storm and the Hurricanes, and I'd sing for them sometimes and eventually with all of the well-known Liverpool bands, including The Big Three, The Fourmost and Gerry and the Pacemakers. I'd do Richie's Mum's hair, always thinking that if I didn't become a star, I could fall back on hairdressing! A plan was hatched for me to sing with The Beatles at the Majestic in Birkenhead, so Brian Epstein could audition me. I thanked Ringo for that and he said: "Why would I have told Brian Epstein about you? It was John Lennon who mentioned you." I was astounded. John and I weren't close. He was a man's man and quite shy, and that's where I believe his caustic sense of humour came from.

Thanks to John, I had this fabulous opportunity to be signed by The Beatles' own manager and I blew it. I sang Summertime at my audition; in the wrong key because I hadn't rehearsed it. I walked straight off the stage and got the next ferry home. I knew I was bad. I had no choice but to put that behind me and

carry on: working and singing where I could. Later on, I was singing at the Blue Angel coffee shop with John Reuben's modern jazz group, completely unaware that Brian was once again in the audience. This time I was relaxed, singing some of my favourites like Della Reese's Bye Bye Blackbird. Brian came up to me after and said: "Why didn't you sing like that the first time?" He was trying to sign me the next day, and on September 6, 1963, he succeeded.

Things moved so quickly. A few weeks later, I took time off from my job to go to London and record a song with the brilliant music producer George Martin, Love of the Loved, written by Lennon and McCartney, and released it as my first single on September 27, 1963. Brian had already persuaded George to see me sing at The Cavern, and he seemed to have enjoyed my interpretation of Peggy Lee's Fever. George not only produced The Beatles but also Shirley Bassey and Matt Munro. He invited me to London and I did a second audition with him backed by musos at the famous Abbey Road Studios. Brian, usually so cool, took me to a pub and kept urging me to have a brandy, but it was him who was nervous, not me. I did the audition, and when I came out I saw my father.

He'd come all the way to London to check on me but made out he was just paying a visit! Brian had put me up in a hotel during this time and it took a couple of days after the second audition before I knew that the recording deal with George and Parlophone was in the bag. I knew when a bottle of champagne arrived in my room with a card around the neck. "Congratulations!" it read, "the Blackbird has landed!"

As soon as I got back home, I handed in my notice. I told the boss: "I'm leaving because I'm going to be a star!" The girls clubbed together and bought me a vanity case in cream leather, suitable for a diva, and I still have it. Within weeks, I was setting off on my first UK concert tour with Gerry and the Pacemakers.

The fun of those early days in Liverpool is still deep inside me. I'd lived and breathed rock'n'roll since I first heard Bill Haley and the Comets when I was 11 or 12. At 16, I had my job as a clerk-typist, then at lunchtimes I had a small job checking in coats at the Cavern. Bands would play at lunchtimes as well as the evenings. The pay was poor but they gave me my lunch and as a bonus I saw The Beatles play. How good was that! I got a soup and a roll: I can still taste it now, everything tasted of disinfectant. In the evenings

I'd go to the Zodiac club and serve coffees, and when anyone would let me, I was singing.

We lived above George Murray's Barbers Shop on Scotland Road. Dad's nickname was Shiner because his boots were so beautifully polished, you could see your face in them. Mam sold secondhand clothes at the market. She used to claim my singing talent came from the Welsh side of her family, and she did have a wonderful soprano voice. My Dad begged to differ: he was Irish Catholic and claimed it came from his side. After a few jars on a Saturday night, people would come back to our flat to do a turn. We all loved music. My brother George loved Frank Sinatra and Jim Reeves, and John loved jazz — he played the clarinet and saxophone. Even when I was very small, someone would spot me and put me on the kitchen table and I invariably got a round of applause for singing.

My biggest musical influences were Della Reese, Dinah Washington and Sam Cooke. We all loved American artists and we all knew someone who went away to sea and would bring records back from New York. As a teenager, my favourites were Frankie Lymon and the Teenagers, simply because I could sing in his key as his voice hadn't broken yet. The B-side of his single, Why

Left: on a motorbike with friends in the late 1950s. Above: a young Bobby Willis — Cilla's future husband

—9—

Do Fools Fall In Love, was I'm Not A Juvenile Delinquent. The lyric was just one long no, no, no, no that I never stopped singing. My family were great, they never once complained.

I had a one-track mind. All I wanted to do was sing and be famous. There had been the occasional boyfriend but none that made any real impression. Then at 17, I met Bobby Willis. I couldn't know what he'd eventually mean to me; it wasn't obvious at the time. I first met him when I was at the Zodiac. I was with my friend Pat Davies, and we saw two of them: Bobby and his great friend, Alan, and they both had suntans. They looked wonderful; we thought they were foreign, possibly Swedish, because Bobby had a shock of blond hair. I was so disappointed to learn he was from Liverpool. That night he told me he was 21, had his own car and that his dad owned a bakery. All lies. He was 19, worked at the bakery in Woolworths, and didn't own a car. Despite that, we hit it off, though it was never plain sailing. I was incredibly young. He gave us lifts in a Crawford's biscuit van that was barely roadworthy.

My parents had two sayings: one life, you've got to live it, and you've got to do better than us. I had wanted to work in the cigarette factory or sugar factory be-

cause all my friends were there but my mother had different ideas for me. When I left school at 15 she and my dad supported me through commercial college until I got my short-lived office job.

None of us could have imagined the impact of the success of Anyone Who Had a Heart. I was in demand everywhere: all the new, cool programmes like Juke Box Jury and Ready Steady Go, presented by the lovely Cathy McGowan. She and I became great friends. She was down-to-earth and Catholic like me. She knew what was "in" and "out" and had a great sense of style: we loved shopping together. We'd spend a fortune on miniskirts and dresses! I even did The Beatles Christmas show at the Astoria Theatre in Finsbury Park, London at the end of 1963. Billy J. Kramer, Gerry and the Pacemakers, The Fourmost and Tommy Quickly were also on the bill, but you couldn't hear anyone because of the screaming Beatles fans! Following that early chart success, I did 400 live performances in eight months.

Brian had also got me a run at the London Palladium in a show called Startime with Frankie Vaughan and Tommy Cooper. He told me it would last four weeks. It lasted nine months. I had some great laughs but was

working all week and didn't relish doing three shows on a Saturday, and I'd also work on a Sunday. I was making up my money so I could pay off my debt to Brian Epstein, who'd invested a lot in me at the beginning. I was on £350 a week for 13 shows. It was an incredible time. Though I didn't realise, I was also learning stagecraft and timing from two masters. I owe my whole career to that nine months.

I fell in love with Frankie Vaughan. Well, wouldn't I just. He was very patient with me. I'd knock on his door in between houses and make any excuse to be with him. He was suave, debonair. Tommy Cooper was totally different. I never saw him, except on stage, in trousers. He wandered about in suspenders holding up his socks, long underpants and a shirt. I was a pest. With Brian, I'd complain about the Palladium and ask him why he hadn't got me a booking at the Liverpool Empire instead! Living in London had been difficult for me, but that was really because I wasn't seeing the real cosmopolitan London. I was living in hotels.

I remember the Palladium doorman George predicting I'd do the Royal Variety Show at the end of 1964. I thought he was being ridiculous: I'd only been professional five minutes but he was totally right. By the time I did, my photo was 10ft tall outside the theatre. When the moment came to meet the Queen, the lovely Millicent Martin, who had become famous singing in the satirical review That Was the Week That Was, had taken me through my paces and taught me the etiquette of the situation: how to curtsey and to address royalty. It was an incredible line-up, including Noël Coward, Eric Morecambe and Ernie Wise, Millicent and Bob Newhart. I was wearing shocking-pink gloves up to my elbow — you couldn't do flesh on flesh with the Queen — and when it came to my turn in the line-up, she said to me, what are you doing at the moment? I thought, everyone knows what I'm doing at the moment: have you not seen that great big photograph outside? But I was very courteous. Millicent had pointed out to me that the Queen was a very busy lady and might not know too much about me. Fatal. I gave the Queen such earache. I gave her so much information she went, "Well done" and moved on without asking another question. When she came to Tommy Cooper, he asked her if she was going to the cup final at Wembley that year. When she said sadly, she couldn't, he said: "That's a great shame. Can I have your ticket?"

When I look back, I was so naive. In the clubs I sang as Swinging Cilla and I thought everyone adored me, but now I can see that it was because I was singing with bands like The Beatles and everyone thought they could meet them through me. I became rich very young and it was the family and Bobby who kept my feet on the ground. I remember driving back to Liverpool through the night from the Palladium and I had got really bigheaded. I was sitting in my dad's chair and he just took one look at me and said: "You, Up." My mother went to bingo and he went down the pub and I was left with Lassie the dog watching telly. They weren't going to change their lives just because their daughter was famous. It was an eye-opener. They were going out of their way to show they weren't going to change their routine. I appreciate it to this day.

The first thing I wanted to do when I made money was to buy my parents a house. I remember seeing my mother in tears once, she so desperately wanted her own council house. Well, her own front door would have been enough. We had to get into the flat through the back yard where we kept the coal and where the outside toilet was. The minute I got a few bob, not only did we have a front door but a detached house in Woolton Village with front and back gardens, two bathrooms and three bedrooms. But she still complained: "Couldn't you have bought me a house with a bus stop outside. I've got to walk up that hill there..."

I didn't think twice about any of it at the beginning. The Beatles, Gerry and the Pacemakers and all these other Liverpool bands had made it before me. I felt very much alone. It was new territory for girls. I followed Helen Shapiro, and Lulu came along soon after.

I had no idea what I was doing at first on television. I was shy, not flamboyant like Shirley Bassey. Bobby said to me, if it's not natural to move your arms around, just stand there and let the voice do the talking — and he was right. Even now I can't walk into a roomful of people on my own but when I'm performing, as soon as I see the red light, I'm like Red Rum: you have to hold me back.

It was only three short months from Brian calling me in the phone box in Liverpool to let me know that Anyone Who Had A Heart was a No 1 hit to my 21st birthday. By that time I'd also released a second single, You're My World, which achieved a consecutive No 1 for me in the charts on May 1, just a few weeks before my birthday. To celebrate, Brian took me to the restaurant now called Le Caprice for lunch with Bobby and George Harrison. Because I was also working two shows a day at the Palladium, I went to a very early lunch and Brian ordered wild strawberries in brandy because he knew I wouldn't eat it and he wanted it! The birthday celebrations continued at Brian's home. From there, I rang my mother in Liverpool — they had a phone by then— and they were having a birthday do without me and everybody was there, all my aunties, and I could hear this music blaring out. Well, I put the phone down and cried my eyes out. I never told her.

It had been an extraordinary year. I will never forget what Brian told the press, after Anyone Who Had A Heart reached No 1, about hearing me sing at the Blue Angel club: "...she looked magnificent — a slender, graceful creature with the ability to shed her mood of dignified repose when she was singing a fast number. I was convinced from that moment that she could become a wonderful artiste, and I was right. She's a beautiful lady from whom we can all learn something. She is what she is: an untutored girl from a working-class family in a lowly part of Liverpool. She's not easily intimidated by anything or anyone."

Now it was up to the Liverpool girl to make the most of what she had been given ■

Opposite: at a friend's house in the early 1960s

—12—

"My best friend Pat and I loved the Cavern, and I worked in the cloakroom during the day. Here we are sitting stage right, just in front of the dressing room where all the groups got changed"

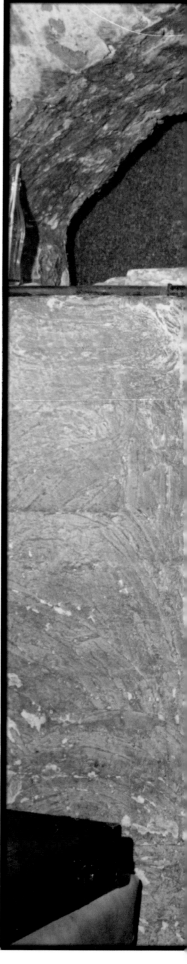

Chatting to Pat Davies at the Cavern club in Liverpool in April 1963. The Beatles had a residency there, so Cilla, determined to break into showbusiness, got a part-time job at the club as a cloakroom attendant

"I'd do Ringo's mum's hair, always thinking that if I didn't become a star, I could fall back on hairdressing!"

After spending Christmas Day 1963 with friends and family in Liverpool, Ringo and Cilla charter a flight to take them back to the capital

All smiles behind the camera at ABC TV Studios, in 1964

Traffic-stopper: Cilla with a framed image of The Beatles, in London, 1964

Feathers and sequins: Cilla flaunts her figure in a costume for Night Of 100 Stars at the London Palladium, 1964

Shorn in a teacup: Cilla has her hair done at Vidal Sassoon, London, April 1964

The birthday girl: celebrating her 21st, with her mother, also called Cilla, and the family dog, Lassie, in London, May 27, 1964

The icing on the cake: Cilla and Brian Epstein at her 21st birthday party

"When I first met Brian he was wearing a navy-blue cashmere coat and a silk-spotted scarf. I thought, he's gorgeous"

A proud Cilla and Brian Epstein, with the silver disc awarded for her 1964 No 1 single, Anyone Who Had A Heart

Kiss me quick: Billy J. Kramer, Gerry Marsden and Cilla with their silver discs

STOP PRESS!

CILLA BLACK JOINS UPCOMING GERRY AND THE PACEMAKERS TOUR

Within days of the release of her first Parlophone single "LOVE OF THE LOVED" songstress CILLA BLACK will join a nationwide stage tour to be presented by promoter Arthur Howes.   These are the venues and dates:-

FRIDAY	4 OCTOBER	....	Odeon LEWISHAM
SATURDAY	5 OCTOBER	....	Gaumont SOUTHAMPTON
SUNDAY	6 OCTOBER	....	De Montfort Hall LEICESTER
MONDAY	7 OCTOBER	....	Granada WALTHAMSTOW
TUESDAY	8 OCTOBER	....	ABC HUDDERSFIELD
WEDNESDAY	9 OCTOBER	....	Ardwick Apollo MANCHESTER
THURSDAY	10 OCTOBER	....	Adelphi DUBLIN
FRIDAY	11 OCTOBER	....	ABC BELFAST
SATURDAY	12 OCTOBER	....	Colston Hall BRISTOL
SUNDAY	13 OCTOBER	....	Coventry Theatre COVENTRY
TUESDAY	15 OCTOBER	....	Guildhall PORTSMOUTH
WEDNESDAY	16 OCTOBER	....	Rialto YORK
THURSDAY	17 OCTOBER	....	Odeon BOLTON
FRIDAY	18 OCTOBER	....	Odeon LEEDS
SATURDAY	19 OCTOBER	....	City Hall SHEFFIELD
SUNDAY	20 OCTOBER	....	Hippodrome BIRMINGHAM
MONDAY	21 OCTOBER	....	Adelphi SLOUGH
WEDNESDAY	23 OCTOBER	....	Granada HARROW
THURSDAY	24 OCTOBER	....	Granada KINGSTON
FRIDAY	25 OCTOBER	....	Granada WOOLWICH
SATURDAY	26 OCTOBER	....	Odeon COLCHESTER
SUNDAY	27 OCTOBER	....	ABC LUTON
TUESDAY	29 OCTOBER	....	Granada MAIDSTONE
WEDNESDAY	30 OCTOBER	....	ABC CROYDON
THURSDAY	31 OCTOBER	....	ABC CAMBRIDGE
FRIDAY	1 NOVEMBER	......	ABC LINCOLN
SATURDAY	2 NOVEMBER	......	Empire SUNDERLAND
SUNDAY	3 NOVEMBER	......	Empire LIVERPOOL

With Compliments from

Tony Barrow

Press & Public Relations Officer

Nems Enterprises Ltd.
Service House (1st Floor),
13 Monmouth Street,
LONDON, W.C.2.

Telephone: COVent Garden 2332

The original press release announcing Cilla's first UK concert tour with Gerry and the Pacemakers, 1963

"It was hard work touring but the lads looked after me and Billy J. Kramer was no exception"

Climbing the ladder:
Cilla with fellow Liverpudlian
songster Billy J. Kramer, in 1964

In the recording booth at London's Abbey Road Studios with her producer George Martin, April 1964

*Abbey Road Studios, 1964. Top: recording her No 1 hit
You're My World. Bobby Willis and George Martin
are in the background, returning to the control booth.
Centre: with Bobby and George. Bottom: in the
recording booth with George Martin*

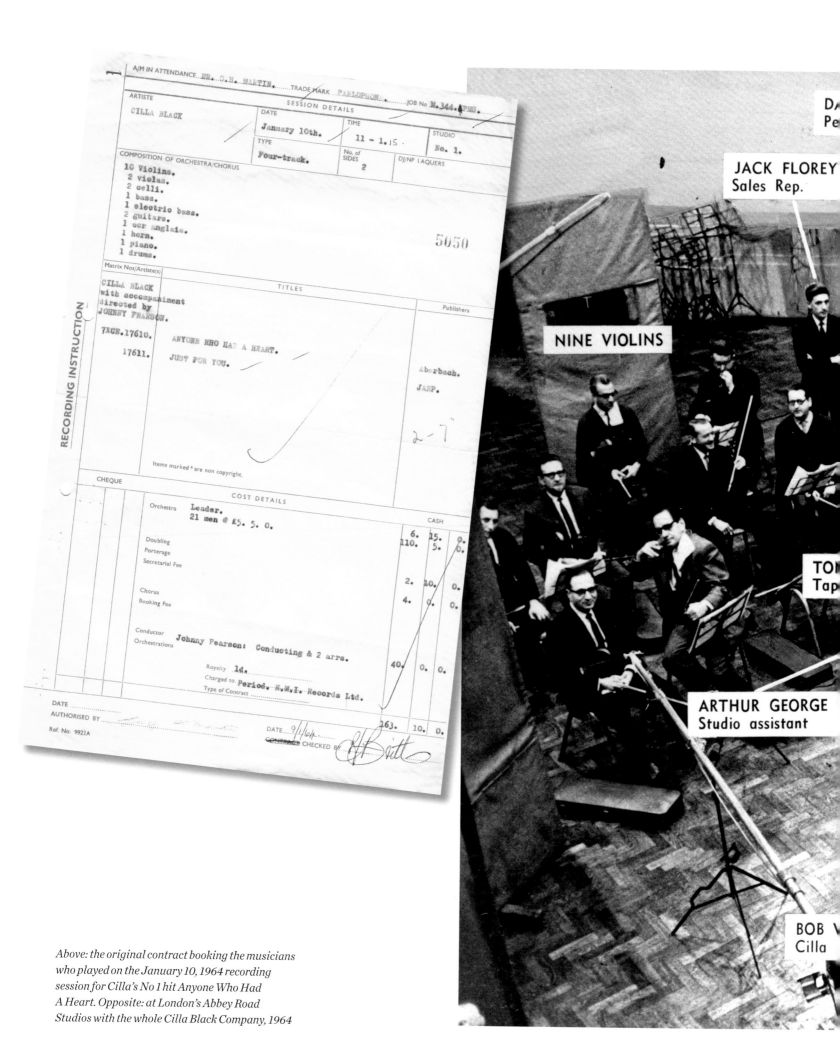

Above: the original contract booking the musicians who played on the January 10, 1964 recording session for Cilla's No 1 hit Anyone Who Had A Heart. Opposite: at London's Abbey Road Studios with the whole Cilla Black Company, 1964

ARAMOR
Appearances

MAL THOMPSON
Exploitation

FRED EXON
Marketing

STEPHEN WRIGHT
Sales and Advertising

NEVIL SKRIMSHIRE
Luxembourg Planner

EDWARD YELLAND
Export Distribution

JOHN MEW
Display

SUSAN CLISTON
Luxembourg Assist.

RON DUNTON
Sleeve Production

TWO 'CELLOS

FRED PEARSON
Press and Publicity

JD PROCTOR
ead Guitar

TWO VIOLAS

STUART ELTHAM
Sound Engineer

GEORGE MARTIN
Recording Manager

RHYTHM and PERCUSSION

IDGE
rator

GEORGE BARNETT
Technical Engineer

ORGAN

CILLA BLACK

JOHNNY PEARSON
Musical Director

s manager

—33—

Strike a pose: Millicent Martin, Cilla, Susan Hampshire and Sylvia Syms at rehearsals for their chorus-girl act for Night Of 100 Stars at the London Palladium, 1964

Royal
Performance
in the presence of
Her Majesty
The Queen
on the Evening of
Monday, November 2ⁿᵈ 1964
at
The Palladium,
London.

Right: chatting on the stairs during rehearsals for a Royal Variety Performance at the London Palladium, with fellow singers Millicent Martin (left), Kathy Kirby (second from left) and Brenda Lee (right), November 1964

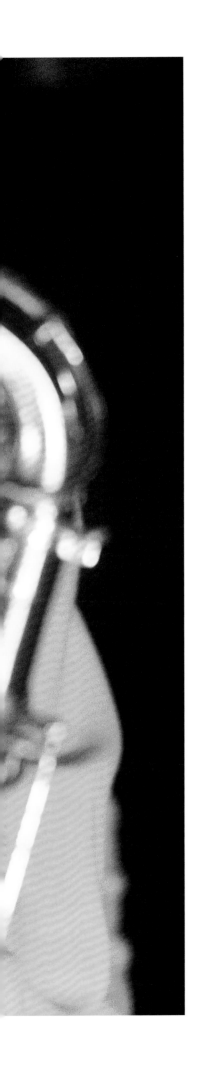

CILLA BLACK

stereo

Cilla

Opposite: sunny and sweet, in 1964.
Above: Cilla wearing a Biba dress on the cover of her
debut album for Parlophone Records, 1965

NEW YORK, DANCING WITH CHIMPS, AND GETTING HITCHED

Above: on The Ed Sullivan Show. Right: sitting pretty on the rocks in New York, 1965

My success had been so meteoric in Britain and The Beatles were doing so well in America, it was inevitable I'd find myself there. In the summer of 1965, when The Beatles were playing Shea Stadium, I was singing in the Persian Room of the five-star Plaza Hotel, New York. It was a very snooty hotel and they didn't really want "our kind" there. The Beatles weren't allowed in, so I had to visit them some place downtown. When they went home I was a bit of a wuss and didn't stick it out. I wasn't prepared to live in America for six months in the hope that something might take off. I missed my parents and I lost my grandmother when I was in the States, and my mother didn't tell me until I got home. That really upset me. I was very close to my Nanna.

Nevertheless, in the time I was there I did the Ed Sullivan show three times with an audience of 80 million. Bob Precht, the producer, was Ed's son-in-law and he took a shine to me and kept inviting me back. The first time I did the show was with The Beatles. I remember George Harrison saying to me in the lift: "I can see you're nervous, Cilla, but just think of it as the Billy Cotton Band Show at home." I tried to give Ed Sullivan as much information as I could and he still introduced me as a Welsh singer! It was a live show and one night I followed a chimp act. It was fine in rehearsals but they couldn't get the right shots so they wanted to make the animal ring smaller. Well, if you're an animal and you're used to a bigger space, you can't make it 3ft smaller and expect everything to be OK. The chimps started ripping their clothes off and doing dreadful things to each other and I could hear: cue the singer, cue the singer. It was the biggest show of the time, broadcast through the Bible Belt, and these chimps were doing unforgettable things to each other while I was trying to sing Dancing In The Street. They should have renamed it Dancing With The Chimps!

Bobby and I had been slowly getting closer. Over the years we had dated, argued, got back together again. He'd been working for Brian as my road manager, driving me to gigs in his Humber Sceptre, but we weren't exclusive for a long time. In America, Brian had at first given me female chaperones, and that really didn't work. I'd end up looking after them, so Bobby also took on that role. After the States, it became clear to us that we didn't want to be apart and we moved in together, renting a beautiful little cottage in Prince Albert Terrace Mews, close to Regent's Park in London. Bobby was also a great songwriter and wrote the B-side of my very first single, Shy Of Love. I remember Brian Epstein offering him £150 for it and I was well impressed with Bobby when he turned it down. He knew that wasn't the right future for him. He was very canny. We were encouraged to keep quiet about the growing relationship. Brian believed all his stars would lose their fans if they knew they were married or dating someone. John Lennon eventually put a stop to it when his son Julian was a year old and none of his fans knew he was married to Cynthia. In the end, he told Brian it was ridiculous.

As Brian's business expanded, it became harder for me to see him, and Bobby had started to make all the decisions for me. In the end we had to discuss the situation with Brian because it had reached the point where I was considering Bobby taking over as my manager. NEMS Enterprises looked after all the stars: The Beatles, Billy J. Kramer, Gerry and the Pacemakers, and more. It was a vast stable in which I was the only filly. We went to Brian's home in Chapel Street to discuss it with him and had a lovely roast-lamb lunch and went on the roof terrace for drinks and coffees. In retrospect, it was terribly sad. I was nearly in tears because Brian was saying, please give me another chance — I promise I'll spend more time with you. Of course I wanted that, we'd always had a terrific bond, but I wanted to think about it. Soon after I was going on a little holiday to Portugal and he met me at Euston before I set

off. He was very excited about a new TV programme he had been negotiating for me with the BBC.

It wasn't long after when I was in a night club overlooking the Gulf of Cadiz with Bobby, Tom Jones and his wife that a waiter came over and said point-blank in broken English: "Your manager is dead." Tom went to find out what was going on. He came back saying the radio was playing early Beatles songs and, yes, it's true. I got home the next day and went straight to Liverpool and on to the funeral at the Jewish cemetery, Long Lane, Aintree. The Beatles didn't go to the funeral because it would have created chaos, it would have turned into Beatlemania, but I did. It was the first time I'd been to a Jewish funeral. His mother, Queenie, was clinging to the coffin. We never saw him buried. It still upsets me terribly today. I adored him. And the selfish thing was, I found myself saying: "What's to become of me now?" I've never forgiven myself for that.

It was a terribly sad time. The coroner recorded an open verdict. Brian had been drinking and taking sleeping tablets. I have never believed for a moment that he took his own life. When I look back I do think he can't have been happy. He was gay at a time when homosexuality was still illegal.

He didn't leave a suicide note, and that would have been totally unlike Brian, believe me! I'd never seen him the worse for wear. But he was under pressure. Things were changing. The Beatles were tired of going on tour and playing concerts where you couldn't hear them because of the continuous screaming from fans. It made more sense to make albums instead. They wrote such brilliant songs. They were spending more time in the recording studio, and as a result they changed the face of recording. I was used to going into a studio and doing an A-side, a B-side for a single, and one for the album in three hours. They were taking over Abbey Road studios and staying there all night, really getting into the technical side — so much so that George Martin used to leave them to it.

When Brian died, he had all kinds of papers on his bed, including a new contract for my first TV show, Cilla. The show established me as an all-round entertainer and its theme tune, Step Inside Love, written for me by Paul McCartney, gave me another hit single. That show went on to attract 22 million viewers and ran until 1976.

I'd been through so much with Brian, had such fun with him, and he was always very protective. I remember the first time I heard about the Ad-Lib club in London, Brian said, "I know I'm going to regret bringing you here," and he was totally right. It was a club that catered for rock'n'roll people in a Soho penthouse — and I loved it. Fur-covered walls, recessed lighting, low tables and large mirrors. The Rolling Stones, The Animals, The Hollies, The Moody Blues and The Beatles hung out there along with up-and-coming names like Mary Quant, Vidal Sassoon, David Bailey, Terry O'Neill, Terence Stamp and Michael Caine. A few years ago, I went to the wedding of Jo and Ronnie Wood's daughter, Leah, and I couldn't take my eyes off Keith Richards. I caught him looking at me and I blurted out: "I didn't half fancy you all those years ago at the Ad-Lib club!" And he went, "Mmm," with the bandana on, "so, what happened?" Well, time happened! When I think about it, he was quite beautiful, more so than Mick Jagger. Well, Mick had those lips, didn't he?

I'd fancied Paul and John from The Beatles and Pete Best when he was originally in the band, he was gorgeous. But never my friend Ringo! But these crushes came and went. Bobby was the only boyfriend I came back to. I remember being in a hotel in Birmingham and Omar Sharif sent me the biggest display of flowers ever. I was filming Work is a Four-Letter Word at the time, directed by Peter Hall, and Omar invited me for tea. Bobby never even allowed me to reply and say thank you!

Making films was part of the madness of the time. I'd had a small part in Ferry Cross the Mersey with Gerry and the Pacemakers. This film was something else again. The cast were all Shakespearean actors and I was not only not Shakespearean trained, I was a non-actor. At that age, you have incredible faith in people and what they say you can do, when they would never dream of doing it themselves. Not any more. I now think twice but then I had so much faith in Brian Epstein that if he'd said you can climb Mount Everest, I'd have said, where's my haversack, I'm off.

In 1966, my single Alfie was a huge hit. Now I'd released eight singles, six of which had been in the Top Ten, in just two years. There's a great picture of me with Pattie Boyd at the premiere of the Alfie film. I looked so relaxed, but if you take a closer look at the photo, I've got a claw-like grip on her hand because I was so nervous. I was wearing a Jean Varon outfit, which I now think didn't look right.

I was also in a review show, Way Out In Piccadilly, at the Prince of Wales Theatre with Frankie Howerd. We were friends until the day he died. Frankie didn't make friends easily, but when he did you knew he would be a friend for life. This little upstart had come in and he was very aware that I would try and steal the show. It was tempting but I looked at Frankie and thought, no, I won't even try. Frankie used to giggle a lot and forget his lines, and blame me, and I used to take it because I had so much respect for him. I learnt so much. It was so sad to hear him say that if he could have taken a pill that would have stopped him being gay, he would have. We loved him exactly as he was. In the show we did sketches together and I opened the show with him and did dance routines. Eric Sykes was directing, and Ray Galton and Alan Simpson, who wrote Steptoe and Son, were the writers. I celebrated my 24th birthday in the show — and Brian put Happy Birthday Cilla up in lights on above Piccadilly Cir-

cus to celebrate! It was fabulous. I stayed there for eight months and left because I needed to get back to singing and wanted to tour Australia, New Zealand and Hong Kong. I'm forever grateful for what I learnt on the stage and for being in these long runs, but I was a solo singer and that's all I ever wanted to be. It was important to get back on the road.

It wasn't until around 1967 that I realised I was a millionairess. In time it became clear that after The Beatles, I would become the biggest-selling artist to come out of Liverpool. Bobby had this Jaguar and I'm round at Brian's and I say: "Well, you've got a Bentley and The Beatles have all got Rolls-Royces... why haven't I got one?" "Well, you can have one," he said. I had an order in on a Jaguar and lost around £500 on it because I cancelled it. Brian insisted I had to have a Bentley, "the Princess of the road". I had never taken any notice of business. A turning point came when Bobby came back home one day after renegotiating a TV contract for me and snapped: "You don't realise what I've been through today. Imagine you're a packet of Persil. I've had to sell you. You are a brand." I had never thought of myself that way before.

Romance did take a backseat to working. Bobby

and I were always splitting up and getting back together again before we got married. Once we got married, everything changed. It was commitment time. I didn't meet anyone I wanted to be with more than Bobby. Even when I went out with other men, I kept thinking it wasn't enough. I thought there was something wrong with me and I would never settle down. Is this all there is, I used to think, this need to be famous? But then when I married Bobby I realised I could have it all. Showbusiness is the only business where a woman can. I was topping the bill with men beneath me and they were all great: they never made me feel I wasn't worthy of it. Because you know what, it was my name up there and I was making money. I put bums on seats.

My proposal wasn't very romantic. Bobby was a very generous man and after we finished recording Cilla, he would take whoever was on the programme, production people, and the stars, out to dinner. On this particular evening we were having another one of our arguments, and Peter Brown, who had been a friend of ours in Liverpool (and is still close to me today) and had arranged John Lennon and Yoko's wedding, said: "You two sound like an old married cou-

Filming her TV show
Cilla at BBC Television
Centre in West London, 1969

Above: tinkling the ivories with Bobby in between recording sessions at Abbey Road Studios, 1964. Opposite: kimono-clad for a production of Way Out In Piccadilly, at the Prince of Wales Theatre, London, November 1966

ple, why don't you get married?"` Bobby said: "Well, you arrange it, Mr Fixit, and we'll do it!" That was my proposal. We'd never really talked about it. Peter turned up to the flat we'd moved to in Portland Place the next day. He was on his way to Marylebone Registry Office to put the banners up... I thought, bloody hell, I'm getting married. I rang Cathy McGowan and told her I was getting married in 48 hours!

I was back in the rehearsal room the Sunday after the wedding. In our lunch break, Bobby took everyone for a drink in the pub across the road. I was happy with it that way. I was in the public eye and a big wedding would have felt like a show anyway, so I thought this was the best way of doing it. The plan was to tell our parents afterwards but word got out before of course. My family were upset but came round. Bobby's complained that they had been done out of a do and out of a wedding and they wanted it! His background was Protestant, mine Catholic. After that it was all systems go. My mother wanted a blessing for me in Liverpool Cathedral or nothing else. Given I had been "living in sin", that wasn't possible but we were very happy with the local parish church in Woolton. But we always kept the day we got mar-

ried in Marylebone Registry Office as our anniversary — Bobby's 27th birthday on January 25, 1969, with Peter Brown as the best man.

Peter's still looking after me today and he invited me to New York to celebrate my 70th birthday. I met him when I was 14 and he was working in Lewis's in Liverpool in the record department. You could ask for a record and listen to it in a booth, and I kept asking him for Frankie Lymon. I was asking for it to be played over and over. He was stacking the shelves in a brown overall (he denies all this) and eventually he said: "Are you going to buy this record or not. If you're not going to buy it, just get out!" He was up and down the ladder like a whore's drawers stacking LPs! I didn't realise then that he was a friend of Brian Epstein, and went to work for him at NEMS. It was a very small world.

Just over a year later, in April 1970, it was clear that all of us who had found fame and fortune with Brian Epstein were moving into a new decade and a new world. The Fab Four finally announced they were splitting up. The Sixties were finally over, and it would never be the same for any of us again. It would, however, continue to be fascinating ∎

Not me, officer: posing with
New York policemen, 1965

"The lovely George Martin and me with my new haircut by Vidal Sassoon"

Deep in conversation with her producer George Martin, in 1965

"I had crushes on all
The Beatles at various times"

*Above and left: John, Paul and Cilla filming The
Music of Lennon and McCartney, November 1965.
Next pages: Cilla with John, Ringo, Paul, the Rolling
Stones' Brian Jones and Donovan at the launch of
Grapefruit's Dear Delilah debut, January 1968*

Previous pages: Cilla with fellow pop stars at the New Musical Express concert in London, April 1965. Among them are Dusty Springfield, The Rolling Stones, Tom Jones, Wayne Fontana, Twinkle and the Ivy League. Left: the lady in white — Cilla takes to the stage, age 21, on the TV show Sunday Night at the London Palladium, April 1965

The Beach Girls: in Portugal with the TV presenter Cathy McGowan

With the singers Petula Clark (centre) and Sandie Shaw (right), in May 1965

"The wonderful Frankie Howerd taught me all I know about comic timing and was such a dear friend"

Frankie Howerd rehearses the Madam Moth scene with Cilla in the show Way Out In Piccadilly, at the Prince of Wales Theatre in London, October 1966

Ooh, I say! Perching on Frankie Howerd's lap, at the Prince Of Wales Theatre, London 1966

With her friend and fellow Parlophone Records' recording star Adam Faith, July 1966.
Next page : dancing on the table — Cilla flaunts her stuff in 1966

"I may look calm on the outside but I am gripping Pattie's hand like a vice at the premiere of Alfie"

Cilla Black, Pattie Boyd and George Harrison at the premiere of the Alfie movie, London 1966

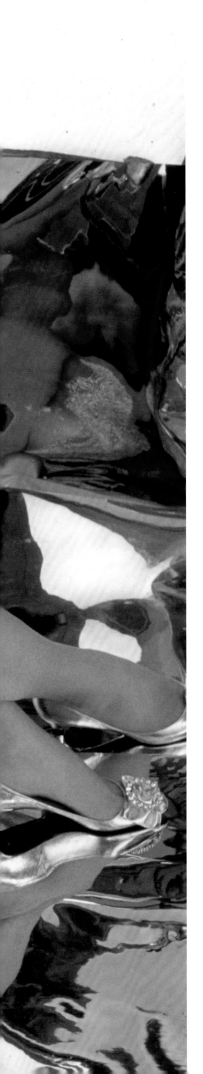

Above: the cover sleeve of Cilla's second album, Cilla Sings A Rainbow, 1966. Her Biba outfit inspired the album's title. The green in her hair is not lighting — Cilla recalls her hairdresser put a slash of green in her locks: "I am the original punk of the Sixties!" Left: another shot taken during the shoot for the album sleeve

Performing at the Savoy in London, 1966 (above), and stylish as ever in matching boots and minidress (opposite)

Right on the dot: Cilla greets fans in Blackpool in a snazzy trouser suit, June 1966

A promotional shot for various record releases, 1967

Cilla enjoys a cuppa after completing the film Work is a Four-Letter Word, 1967. She co-starred in the movie with David Warner

Michael Caine and Julia Foster (left) with Eleanor Bron and Cilla, May 1967

Dedicated follower of fashion: Cilla embraces the 1960s in flared trousers and silver waistcoat (opposite) and pretty in pink (above), 1967

Sheer delight: in the flowing dress she wore for her film Work Is A Four-Letter Word

Working the monochrome look in a 1960s day dress

Above: a promotional picture taken for Cilla's hit break-up single Surround Yourself With Sorrow, 1967

Cilla starred alongside David Warner (left) in the 1968 film Work Is A Four-Letter Word, directed by Peter Hall (right)

On her TV show with Harry H Corbett (left) and Tom Jones — a highlight of the first programme of Cilla's new series for the BBC, January 1968

THE BEST OF CILLA BLACK

Love of the loved
Anyone who had a heart
You're my world (Il Mio Mondo)
You've lost that lovin' feelin'
Love's just a broken heart
Alfie
I only live to love you
What good am I
Step inside love
Where is tomorrow?
Sing a rainbow
It's for you
Yesterday
Goin' out of my head

Above and right: the sleeve for Cilla's first Greatest Hits album, released in 1968. Cilla came up with the idea of the cowgirl look for the photo session

Playing the field: pictures to promote her recordings, c1968

Old pal Ringo Starr appearing on the TV series Cilla

Rehearsing Step Inside Love with Paul McCartney, 1968. McCartney wrote this song, which became the theme tune for Cilla's TV show

Above: the sleeve of Cilla's third album for Parlophone Records,
featuring a radical new hairdo created by the stylist Leslie Russell,
1968. Opposite: another photo taken from the same session

Stamp of approval: Cilla and Cliff count the votes for Britain's song for the Eurovision contest, March 1968

Cilla wrested the top British female singer award from Lulu (right) at an awards ceremony in London, in February 1970. The same evening, Cliff Richard (centre) was voted best-dressed male star

Above: performing with Dusty Springfield in February 1969.
Left: an unused picture taken for the back cover of the 1969 album Surround Yourself With Cilla

Above: feeling the pinch with her friend Bruce Forsyth,1969. Opposte: Cilla in bloom, c1966

Opposite: Cilla and Bobby smile for fans as they leave Marylebone Registry Office in London after their wedding on January 25, 1969. This page: the happy couple enjoy a second ceremony in the Catholic church of St Mary's, Liverpool, January 1969 (top and middle). Bottom: Cilla laughs as Bobby gives his newlyweds speech at the Adelphi Hotel, Liverpool. Next page: Newlyweds Cilla and Bobby party at a friend's flat — Bobby tries out his new cinecamera, while Cilla keeps him on his toes with a carving knife

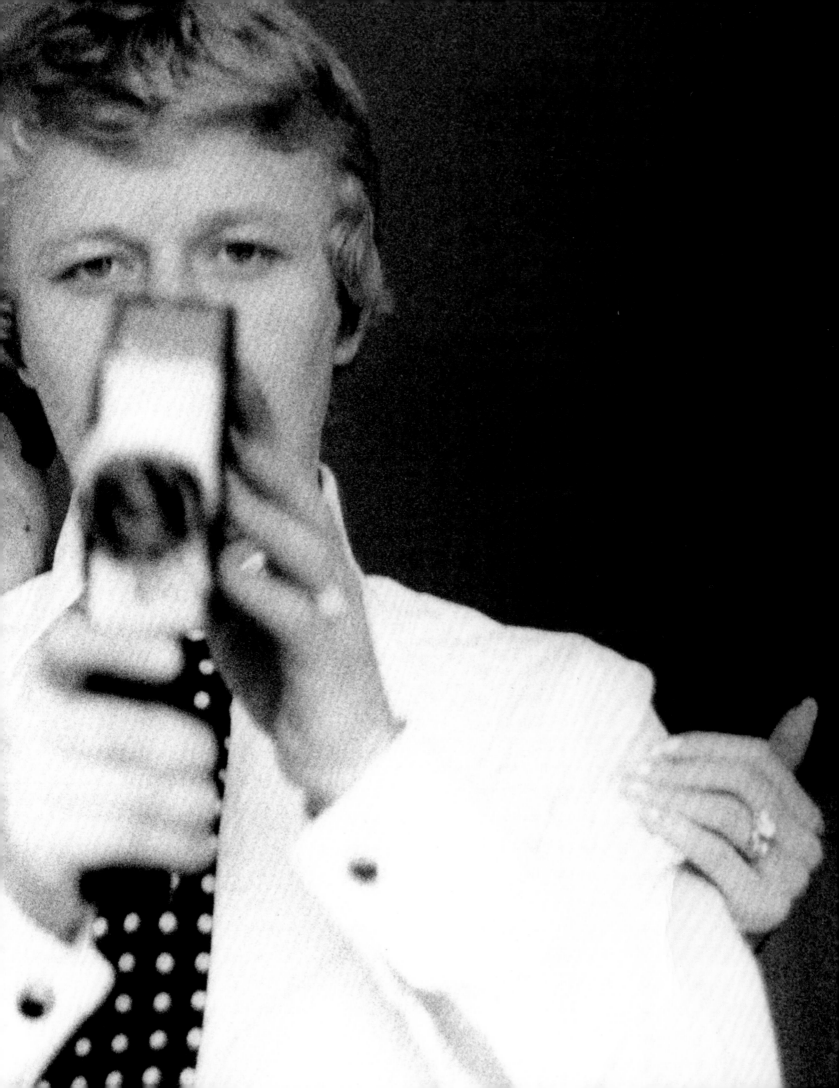

FROM THE SURPRISE OF A FIRST CHILD TO THE SURPRISE! SURPRISE! OF TELEVISION

My first son, Robert, was born in July 1970, just a year after Bobby and I married. There has never been a happier period of my life. It was like the missing piece of a jigsaw finally bringing everything together.

I'd always dreamt of us having a family, and I wanted six children. All my girlfriends in Liverpool had got married and had two or three children years before. It was a different time then. If you weren't married by the time you were 21, you were over the hill. By the time I was married I was quite old, 26. We were living in the flat in Portland Place and the Cilla series was still running. I just knew I couldn't bring a baby up in the West End of London.

We'd heard through a friend of a friend that Lord Birkett's house was up for sale in the Chalfonts, and I remember Bobby leaving to meet him for lunch at San Lorenzo's. Before he went he asked me, do you want this house and I said, yes, I want this house. He seemed so determined but when he came back from lunch, he didn't have the house. He said: "The swine wouldn't come down £5. If he would have come down a fiver, he would have had a deal." I was mortified. I'd heard The Sunday Times had a great property section and I scoured it and found Denham in Buckinghamshire, where I still live to this day. It was perfect and much closer to London. It's an Edwardian eight-bedroom mansion set in 17 acres, originally built for the gin-distilling family, the Gilbeys, in 1912. Today we even have an indoor swimming pool, which the grandchildren love. We saw it on a Friday and Bobby had done the deal by the Sunday. I tried to take six months off after Robert was born, but I was crawling up the walls. By the fourth month, I wanted to get back to work. I needed to be back on tour or singing. I suppose at the time this was not regarded as the done thing. Even having a nanny was unusual. But work was the only thing I'd ever known and I was determined to carry on earning and following my career and to have a family. Robert was joined by his lively brother Ben in April 1974, and our family was complete in October 1980, when Jack was born. There's no doubt they had a lovely childhood. Bobby was determined they would have the best education money could buy. I still regret that my own education wasn't better. The boys went to private school and Jack boarded for a while because we discovered he was dyslex-

ic. Bobby and Paul McCartney used to argue about this in the early days, because all their kids went to state school, but we weren't as clever as Paul really. Both he and John were great academically. I remember saying to my teacher, "Are we a secondary modern school?" and getting the answer: "No, we're just St Anthony's." We didn't even have a title!

I have another child, a daughter. Her name is Ellen. It's still difficult for me to talk about her but she is never forgotten. She was born at seven months and only lived for a couple of hours. The grief was dreadful, I couldn't talk to anyone at the time. I simply locked myself away, then went back to work at the Coventry Theatre just two weeks later. In the weeks and months that followed, things were very dark.

Becoming a parent is full of joys and challenges in your own life and in the lives of those around you. My beloved Dad had died not long after Robert was born. My parents had never moved from the house in Woolton. Mam eventually had to go into a home because her osteoporosis was bad and we kept their house on until long after she died. They had a habit of trying to protect me from anything bad that might be happening at home. When Dad was ill, I know he

used to say, don't worry the girl, don't bring her up here on my account, and the weekend he died, my mother had assured me he was fine and had just had "one of his funny turns". It was my brother John who rang and told me my mother had died. That protection is a very northern thing, which annoys me in a way because they do it to a fault.

Shortly after Jack was born, John Lennon died. I was working in the Arab Emirates and Bobby and I were sunbathing around the pool of a lovely hotel. Bobby overhead someone saying, "Isn't it terrible about John Lennon being shot," and we thought they were doing it deliberately to wind us up. Bobby said, let's go, so we went to our room. I switched on the radio and they were playing Mr Postman and I realised it was true. I was singing John's classic song Imagine in my act, and that night I sang it for him. His first wife, Cynthia, and son, Julian, and I are still friends. Julian's a great photographer as well as a musician, and I try to go whenever they have an exhibition. Cyn's posh but she always rings up in a dead Liverpool accent. She went to art school and was another academic type, like John and Paul, and a very talented artist. She did marvellous etchings for my

That's our boy: Cilla and Bobby with their son Robert. Cilla said, of that time: "There has never been a happier period of my life"

A photo taken to promote Cilla's music projects of the time, 1970

60th birthday. I was never judgmental about John's relationship with Yoko. Yoko was given a hard press. In a magazine interview I commented that you can't help who you fall in love with. She sent me a postcard with a hole in the top and underneath this hole on the postcard were written the words: "This is to see the sky through." Immediately, I went out to the garden and looked through this hole. And I thought, what am I doing? As my 40th birthday loomed, it wasn't too clear which direction I was heading in. I had never stopped working. TV shows and specials, situation comedies, concert tours, panto and summer season shows, I had worked hard and loved it all, but I was looking for something different. You can never tell what's around the corner. When I was much younger, a fortune teller had told me I would be successful until the age of 40, and that thought had been haunting me. Aged 39, I'd done a spot on Top of the Pops, wearing a very short skirt, and shortly after promoted my Best Of Cilla Black album on the Terry Wogan Show. I was full of stories and energy at this point in life and the appearance seemed to capture people's imagination. From that came the offer from LWT for a new

show called Surprise! Surprise! My career didn't end, it simply moved in another direction.

When my 40th birthday did come along, I celebrated it while in the first heady days of my new show. As a surprise to me, Frankie Howerd came out with a birthday cake. He said he'd had to take the candles off it because he was being driven back by the heat! I hate surprises myself, probably because I've given so many of them! I did Surprise! Surprise! for 20 years. I don't know where the time went over that period. We did the programme and specials. I never wearied of it because I wasn't relying on prompts and autocues, I had to learn everything — dates, names, background stories — in case someone on the show had their surprise ruined. In the commercial breaks, I'd be round the back with my producer keeping on top of it all.

There were very moving moments, but it was funny too. Barbara Windsor was on once and we were surprising a 16-year-old boy. When she took him off, I said: "There goes a boy, but he'll come back a man!" But we were caring. If people wanted to meet up after a long time but didn't want to do it on the telly, we arranged for them to do it anyway and we

wouldn't force people to do things that made them feel remotely uncomfortable.

The most memorable surprise for me was a Liverpool one. This guy was in the audience having come over from New Zealand. We were surprising him with all his children and siblings from far-flung places like Abu Dhabi and Hong Kong, you name it. After he'd come all that way and I surprised him, we finished the show and then he collapsed! He'd forgotten to bring his medication and hadn't told our researchers. It was all over the papers the next day. "Never mind Surprise! Surprise!, the show should be called Survive! Survive!" Looking back, it took a lot of stamina, but it was all I knew how to do and to do well. When you do a thing well, you keep wanting to do it better. By 1985 I had also taken on hosting Blind Date. After the first seven programmes were aired, 80,000 people wrote in wanting to participate! At the time the format seemed quite risqué, but it was also fun and didn't humiliate people. Blind Date was to run for a further 18 years.

All through this time, the boys were growing. There were the usual family difficulties to deal with — accidents, the discovery that Jack was dyslexic —

but we all came through it. Being a mother taught me to be patient and more understanding of people, to see their side. When I was a teenager, I couldn't see further than being famous or whatever. Being a mother and indeed a grandmother, you have to listen. It has come to something when my six year-old granddaughter pats me on the head and says, "Well done," when I'm using her computer! Now I'm the student, not the teacher, though that doesn't stop the family coming for advice. As a mother you worry and you worry and you worry — so perhaps I'm glad I didn't have six kids after all! ∎

Hosting her popular TV show
Surprise! Surprise! in 1989

Leaving a London hospital cradling her newborn son, Robert John, August 5, 1970

Wearing aviator sunglasses, hotpants and knee-high boots, Cilla leaves the plane with Robert after a holiday in France

Above: a promo shot for Cilla's 1971 hit single Something Tells Me (Something's Gonna Happen Tonight); *the shot also featured in the souvenir brochure to Cilla's Aladdin pantomime at the London Palladium, 1970. Opposite: relaxing in her dressing room in London, 1970*

"Two redheads together! Boom Boom, Basil Brush, the fox who was a big family favourite in our house"

Cilla with the popular children's TV character Basil Brush in 1970

One of the pictures taken to promote her Sweet Inspiration album, 1970.
"I was so proud of this shot as it was not long after I had my nose done — so I wanted to show it off," says Cilla

An informal photo session at her home in Denham, 1971

Back to Earth: Cilla at Heathrow airport, 1971

Cilla flaunts her socks appeal with Bill Shankly, manager of Liverpool FC

*Previous pages: Cilla alongside the American musician Burt Bacharach on
the Burt Bacharach Show, 1972. Above: the sleeve for Day By Day With
Cilla, 1973 — her final album produced by George Martin, with whom she
had worked for 10 years. The photo session took place in the bedroom at her
Denham home for the cover of the March 1972 edition of TV Times.
Opposite: with her beloved briard dogs Sophie and Ada; the shot was taken
at her Denham home and used on the back sleeve of her album Images, 1971*

Above: celebrating 10 successful years with EMI Records, with Bobby in October 1973.
Opposite: mimicking the joyful pose of her show poster, outside the Palladium, 1973

Above: a very relaxed Cilla — one of a series of pictures taken to promote her concert brochures and publicity material, c1977.
Left: taken during the sixth series of the TV show Cilla. The 1973 shoot later featured in various tour programmes

Above: on the Cilla Black Show, 1974. Opposite: winning an award at London's Grosvenor House in 1975

Left: from a photo session to promote Cilla's Top 20 hits compilation for EMI: The Very Best Of Cilla Black, 1983. Right: from the photo session to promote Cilla's album of 1970s love songs, Especially For You, 1980

Surprise! Surprise! Cilla with her larger-than-life Spitting Image puppet, in 1987

Miss Piggy and Cilla sparkle at the Royal Variety Performance in 1993

"My 30th anniversary, new hairstyle but the same pose!"

Back to the future: Cilla poses with a younger cut-out of herself. Next page: Wonder wall — Cilla returns to the Cavern club in Liverpool, older and wiser, in the 1990s

Life's one big game: Cilla juggling and posing with hoops in the 1990s

Lorra lorra laughs: the actress Barbara Churkin is set up on a blind date with Mr Bean for a charity episode of Blind Date, in 1993

Watching female contestants flaunt their wares on Blind Date, in 1996

"With Alex and Sue at the first Blind Date wedding and of course the infamous hat! Everyone said I looked like one of Ken Dodd's Diddy Men. I love hats but hats hate me!"

Cilla Black beams as she attends the first Blind Date wedding, between Alex and Sue Tatham, in 1991

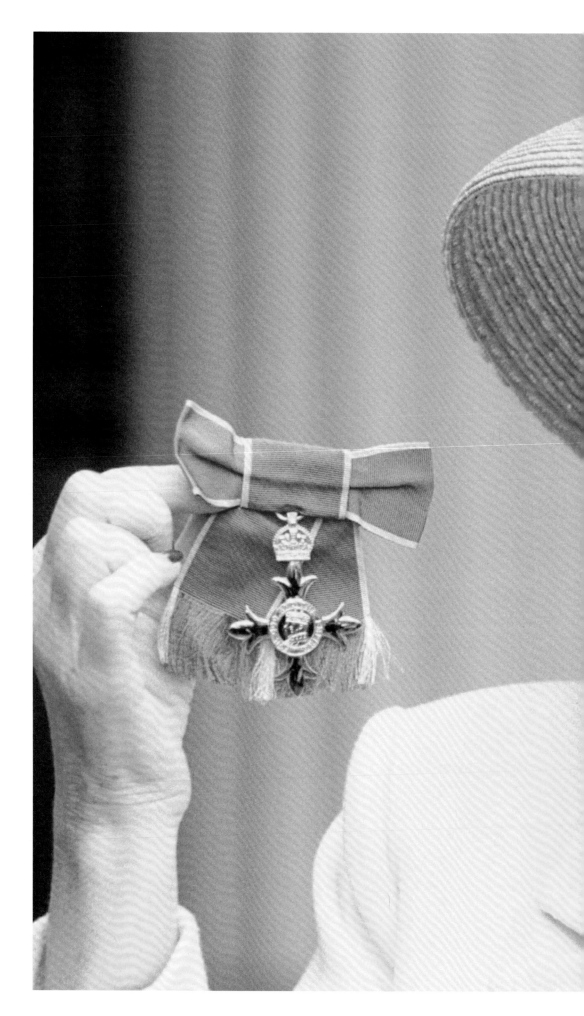

*At her investiture at
Buckingham Palace, 1997*

LEARNING
HOW TO
GO IT ALONE

If a phone call on a cold winter's day in Liverpool in 1964 sealed my fate, so did the final episode of Blind Date, the show I hosted 26 weeks a year for 18 years. I had lost Bobby to cancer three years before, I was approaching 60, and I thought: "I want to stop. This is my time now." I missed Bobby being there in the dressing room in his chair and thought: "What would he do if he was in my shoes?" And I decided he'd think exactly the same as me. He'd say: "Throw in the towel now, what do you need all this for?"

The only way to stop seemed to me to be to announce my departure live on the show. I told nobody except my son Robert, who was by this time organising much of my life and, even then, I'd warned him that I'd have no idea whether I was going to go ahead or not until we started to film.

I told him, if I haven't done it within the first 10 minutes, you'll know my bottle has gone. I had friends in the audience and I was meeting Dale Winton afterwards for dinner, but I told none of them because I didn't know myself. It wasn't until I heard the Blind Date music that I thought: "I'm going for it." I went off autocue and just did my thing, announcing: "This will be my last Blind Date." The audience was looking amazed: what did she just say? It was all in slow motion. Robert was great. He handled all the press. My producer said: "What have you just done?" And I said: "It's not the same without Bobby." Of course I could have gone on, but the point was, I didn't want to.

Bobby was only 57 when he began to be bothered by an irritating cough and tiredness. We had been celebrating our pearl-wedding anniversary in Barbados and after much nagging, he finally agreed to have tests. The news was devastating: he had a cancerous tumour on his liver. Jack was in the middle of his A-levels. Pat [my friend] came straight over from the States. He underwent treatment at the Royal Free in London, but within a few months, on October 22, 1999, he was dead. I'd been massaging his feet at the foot of the bed, the boys were watching Grandstand when Robert noticed that Bobby's oxygen mask was no longer moving. And

at that moment, the room had flooded with light.

There were rumours that we had split up when Bobby stopped appearing with me for the recordings of Blind Date, and really he had been diagnosed with cancer. At the time, the show went on and he wanted it that way because he was very private and proud. Work for me was also a distraction: I was back recording Blind Date just a week after the funeral, but now I've realised the show doesn't have to go on. He made me go and do the shows, and at the end of the day it was like him going to a football match, to see his beloved Liverpool. It was for 90 minutes when he'd forget about everything, and doing the show was like that for me. On the studio floor for two hours, I just forgot about everything and, dare I say it, enjoyed it. I took his advice.

I'd worked every hour God had sent me, and the time had come to live differently. Now I'm really annoyed if anything interferes with my social life! My single friends persuaded me out after Bobby died: they didn't like to think of me going back to Denham alone. I love going to the theatre, meeting friends, and after a lifetime of everything being arranged for me and having Bobby at my side, I love travelling by myself. I used to be terrified. Bobby would try and calm me down each time we flew by saying: "Cilla — I am NOT planning to die in a plane. Have you got that in your head?" Then one day he said: "Of course I might not be planning to die in a plane, but that doesn't mean you might not!" That put me right back to square one. Now I might even treat myself to a trip to Australia soon.

I was very lucky in having such wonderful friends who looked after me in my bereavement. We were a couple, Bobby and I, and we only went out with other couples, so all of a sudden I'm on my own and thought: "It's about time I went out with my single friends." It all started in Barbados with Cliff. He invited me to his house and included me with his friends, and we're very close now. It's funny when I remember being a teenager in Liverpool, who was desperate to catch a glimpse of Cliff when he played at the Philharmonic Hall. I couldn't afford a ticket

and hung about the stage door with my friend Patti, hoping to meet him. He'd sped off in a taxi and I was so daft I hailed a cab and we followed him! And we still didn't see him...

And there were my other male friends: Christopher Biggins, Paul O'Grady (I just call him Savage), Peter Brown and, of course, Dale Winton. I didn't pick these friends because they are gay. It just worked that way. Story of my life!

In the early stages following Bobby's death I felt very alone and I needed to be looked after, but I'm very independent now. I'm also set in my ways. At first I still hoped for romance, but when I think about it, that was only being desperate to fill the void that Bobby had left and nobody is going to do

that. So at this stage of life, I don't want it any other way. I want to have fun. Fun, not a lorra lorra laffs! I never used that catchphrase, but I did capitalise on it. The phrase came from Dustin Gee who used to do an impersonation of me. I did used to say a lorra but I never said a lorra lorra!

I'm also blessed in my female friendships. Pat Davies I met in Liverpool at college. She became a clerk at Littlewoods, and we hung about the Cavern together, always fretting about what we were going to wear and trying to emulate Audrey Hepburn, and I still see her all the time. I'm a year older than her by all of five days, and I say to her, whatever is happening to me now you've got that to look forward to next year, which she hates. She also made her way to

The hugely popular game show Blind Date was presented by Cilla from 1985-2003

London in the Sixties to work for Polydor, using her contacts to organise parties for the record company. She was very influential, a force to be reckoned with, and a great organiser. For a while, Ringo would only work for her at the record company. She now lives in Los Angeles, but as soon as she had heard Bobby had died, she got the first plane over. That's true friendship. She's always looked out for me. I go to visit her at her home, she comes to stay with me in Barbados every year and at my house in Spain. Recently her husband, Jeff — who speaks a bit like John Wayne — said to her: "Patty, just how long is this bereavement going to go on for?" She still makes me laugh. She's full of terrible sayings like: "Well, didn't she put her hand down the toilet and pull out a chocolate bar!"

Then there's Penny, who came to work with me and look after Robert when he was still a baby and she was 18 years old and is still with me now as a housekeeper. She stays all week at the house in Denham and lives with her sister. I don't have to worry about a thing. I tend to live in my flat in London and go home for the weekends, cooking a big roast for the family on a Sunday — Robert, his wife, Fiona, and their children Max and Alana and my other sons.

It's a wonderful life: the only problem I have is turning 70. There's no escaping the fact I'm on the home straight now! But very little fazes me any more. The last time I felt nervous was at the Royal Variety Show in 2001. I was out of my comfort zone, showing much more than I ever imagined. Savage had persuaded me to do a scene from Gypsy, playing an old stripper. He taught me how to bump and grind and walk at the same time. The song was You Gotta Get a Gimmick! There was very little time to rehearse and there I was, playing Miss Electra, wearing an outfit with light bulbs that refused to light all through rehearsal. Savage kept saying: "You've got to sell it! You've got to do the bumps and grinds and do the, Hello Joe, you want to give it a go…" and I thought, I can't do that! I had this guy soldering my outfit trying to make it light up. The lights hadn't been working all day, but as luck would have it on the night, the lights were working and I was also overselling the song because I'd been compensating for the lights earlier in the day. That performance still embarrasses me. I've never seen it.

Two days later, I was due to meet the Queen and the Duke of Edinburgh at Buckingham Palace for a private audience. I was dressed very soberly in grey and she said: "I see you are wearing rather a lot more than you wore the other night!" And my face went red. I blame Savage. I've met the Queen many times over the years and I'm so proud to have been the first woman to have hosted a Royal Variety Performance.

I lost my faith when Bobby got ill. I was brought up a devout Catholic, but stopped going to church in the early days of my success. I used to go to Mass every Sunday, but I found that after Anyone Who Had A Heart made it to No 1 in the charts, people in the congregation would be distracted by me and I stayed away. Bobby had lost his mother when he was 11, lost his father, lost his brother to cancer, and I thought: "What kind of a god is this that would take him at 57 years of age?" And I've not made it up with God even now.

I've had a few admirers since he's gone, but nothing serious. The businessman John Madejski is a true friend today, and helped me through an awful lot in the early stages because I was still grieving over Bobby and very needy. I met John in Barbados at a mutual friends and he knocked a whole glass of red wine over my cream silk skirt and gave me a card saying "call me" and I thought: "What is this?" I never called him, but I did keep the card. It made me giggle because the name of one of his companies was Good Head Productions! It was sometime later when I was in the Caprice with a girlfriend that this man, a stranger, came over to me and said: "You don't remember me, do you?" I looked at him, head to toe and said: "Well, actually, no, I don't!" And then I said: "I bloody do remember, you spilt a glass of red wine over me and all you gave me was a card!" He said: "You never called, and I said: "Well, what am I going to do, call and say my skirt is ruined?" He said: "Well, call me." I said: "You call me!" And it was three weeks later that he called and invited me to Henley and he was fine, not the obnoxious man I thought he was, and he turned out to be an incredible friend.

I'm trying to retire but nobody will let me! I didn't even think about my 50th year in showbusiness until somebody told me it was five decades since I'd been signed by Brian Epstein. I'm aware I've had a very charmed life. At least I can go to my grave being proud of what I've done. Even though I was born without money, I didn't know it. I didn't know the council classed where I lived as a slum; it was my home. How dare anyone talk like that. I didn't see any problem with hand-me-downs. I didn't know any different, and everybody was in the same boat.

I'm grateful for every minute. Television was the icing on the cake in my career, but television found me, I didn't find it. Singing and music are the loves that have driven my life. My headstone should simply say: "Here's Cilla the singer." In the meantime, I know I've had a great guardian angel looking after me throughout my life. I just hope he's a feller! ∎

Left: firm friends Cilla and Paul O'Grady in 2000. Above: big smiles all round — Jerry Hall and Cilla at The Dorchester Club, London, 2000

Wearing her heart on her chest at a Royal Variety Performance in London, November 2001

Continuing her feisty dance routine, performed in front of the Queen

Left and above: making a guest appearance in the West End comedy, The Play What I Wrote, honouring Morecambe and Wise, 2002

Above and opposite: from the photo session promoting Cilla's studio album Beginnings, 2003

Above: celebrating 10 years of the National Lottery, with the boyband Blue at Tate Modern in London, 2004.
Right: Cilla presenting Cilla Live, December 2004

Shirley Bassey, Joan Collins and Cilla at the launch party for Joan's novel, Misfortune's Daughters, London 2004

Terry O'Neill and Cilla at an exhibition of the renowned photographer's work in London, March 2005

Julian Lennon hugs Cilla at the book launch for the biography about his father, John

With Sir George Martin at a book launch for a biography of John Lennon by his first wife, Cynthia Lennon, 2005

Picture taken to promote Cilla's most recent studio album, Beginnings, 2003

Taking a spin around Mayfair with friend Robin Morgan

Rubbing noses with Sir Ian McKellan on the press night for the West End show Acorn Antiques: The Musical, in 2005

Smiling alongside Lord Andrew LLoyd Webber, at the same press night at London's Theatre Royal

Cilla with the businessman John Madejski and John and
Norma Major at an aftershow party in October 2006

Arriving at a wedding reception with Peter Mandelson, December 2006

With her close friend Pattie Boyd, 2007

Cilla and Shirley Bassey (left) at a party for Dame Shirley's 70th birthday, December 2007. Christopher Biggins looks delighted to be in the middle

Surrounded by scantily clad men and women at Shirley Bassey's 70th birthday bash

Celebrating Shirley Bassey's 70th, with Siouxsie Sioux (left) and the designer Pam Hogg

Above, from left: Rolf Harris, Dame Edna Everage, Dame Vera Lynn, Sir Roger Moore, Cilla Black,
Vera's daughter Virginia, Sir Roger Moore's wife Kristina, June Whitfield and Ronnie Corbett
celebrate the 90th birthday of Dame Vera Lynn, in London, March 2007

She shall go to the ball: Cilla gets in the mood for panto season, 2008

A real knees-up: with Tracey Emin, backstage at London Fashion Week's Fashion For Relief show, in 2008

Previous pages: Cilla duets with Barry Manilow on Des O'Connor's Tonight programme, 2008. Right: Strutting her stuff on the catwalk for charity at London Fashion Week, 2008

Above: Cilla sheds a tear during her appearance on Piers Morgan's Life Stories in 2009.
Right: after five decades in showbusiness, Cilla isn't fazed by the limelight

"When Cilla met Harry and what a riot we had!"

A royal knees-up: Prince Harry and Cilla at the inaugural
Sentebale Polo Cup in Barbados, January 2010

Bill Wyman signs a copy of his book Rolling With The Stones for Cilla at a launch party in London

Top: old friends Ronnie Wood (left), Dame Vera Lynn (centre) and Cilla at The Nordoff Robbins Silver Clef Awards, in 2010.
Bottom: Ringo and his wife, Barbara Bach, and Cilla at an exhibition of work by the famous 1960s tailor Tommy Nutter, in 2011

Cilla and Sir Cliff brave the rain at Royal Ascot, June 2011

Not bitter: Keith Lemon ropes in Cilla for his Lemonaid show, 2012.
Next pages: the sleeve of the CD and DVD released by Parlophone Records to celebrate Cilla's 50th anniversary in showbusiness

DISCOGRAPHY 1963-2013

(Researched and compiled by Stephen Munns for www.cillablack.com)

U.K. SINGLES

Release Date	A side b/w B side, Record Label & Catalogue Number	Highest Chart Pos.
27/09/1963	LOVE OF THE LOVED (Parlophone R5065) b/w Shy Of Love	35
31/01/1964	ANYONE WHO HAD A HEART (Parlophone R5101) b/w Just For You	1
01/05/1964	YOU'RE MY WORLD (Parlophone R5133) b/w Suffer Now I Must	1
31/07/1964	IT'S FOR YOU (Parlophone R5162) b/w He Won't Ask Me	7
08/01/1965	YOU'VE LOST THAT LOVIN' FEELIN' (Parlophone R5225) b/w Is It Love?	2
15/04/1965	I'VE BEEN WRONG BEFORE (Parlophone R5269) b/w I Don't Want To Know	17
07/01/1966	LOVE'S JUST A BROKEN HEART (Parlophone R5395) b/w Yesterday	5
25/03/1966	ALFIE (Parlophone R5427) b/w Night Time Is Here	9
03/06/1966	DON'T ANSWER ME (Parlophone R5463) b/w The Right One Is Left	6
14/10/1966	A FOOL AM I (Parlophone R5515) b/w For No One	13
02/06/1967	WHAT GOOD AM I? (Parlophone R5608) b/w Over My Head	24
17/11/1967	I ONLY LIVE TO LOVE YOU (Parlophone R5652) b/w From Now On	26
09/03/1968	STEP INSIDE LOVE (Parlophone R5674) b/w I Couldn't Take My Eyes Off You	8
07/06/1968	WHERE IS TOMORROW? (Parlophone R5706) b/w Work Is A Four-Letter Word	39
07/02/1969	SURROUND YOURSELF WITH SORROW (Parlophone R5759) b/w London Bridge	3
27/06/1969	CONVERSATIONS (Parlophone R5785) b/w Liverpool Lullaby	7
21/11/1969	IF I THOUGHT YOU'D EVER CHANGE YOUR MIND (Parlophone R5820) b/w It Feels So Good	20
04/12/1970	CHILD OF MINE (Parlophone R5879) b/w That's Why I Love You	–
15/11/1971	SOMETHING TELLS ME (SOMETHING'S GONNA HAPPEN TONIGHT) (Parlophone R5924) b/w La La La Lu	3
11/02/1972	THE WORLD I WISH FOR YOU (Parlophone R5938) b/w Down In The City	–
17/11/1972	YOU YOU YOU (Parlophone R5972) b/w Silly Wasn't I?	–
04/01/1974	BABY WE CAN'T GO WRONG (EMI 2107) b/w Someone	36
24/05/1974	I'LL HAVE TO SAY I LOVE YOU IN A SONG (EMI 2169) b/w Never Run Out (Of You)	–
25/10/1974	HE WAS A WRITER (EMI 2227) b/w Anything That You Might Say	–
28/03/1975	ALFIE DARLING (EMI 2278) b/w Little Bit Of Understanding	–
25/07/1975	I'LL TAKE A TANGO (EMI 2328) b/w To Know Him Is To Love Him	–
12/03/1976	LITTLE THINGS MEAN A LOT (EMI 2438) b/w It's Now	–
09/1976	EASY IN YOUR COMPANY (EMI 2532) b/w I Believe (When I Fall In Love, It Will Be Forever)	–
15/07/1977	I WANTED TO CALL IT OFF (EMI 2658) b/w Keep Your Mind On Love	–
12/05/1978	SILLY BOY (EMI 2791) b/w I Couldn't Make My Mind Up	–
22/09/1978	THE OTHER WOMAN (EMI 2840) b/w Opening Night	–
09/1985	THERE'S A NEED IN ME (Towerbell TOW74) b/w You've Lost That Lovin' Feelin'	–
12/1985	SURPRISE, SURPRISE (Towerbell TOW81) b/w Put Your Heart Where Your Love Is	–
06/09/1993	THROUGH THE YEARS (Columbia CD6596982) b/w Through The Years (Orchestral Version), The Feelings Just Get Stronger (Through The Years), Through The Years (Do You Remember?)	54
18/10/1993	HEART AND SOUL with Dusty Springfield (Columbia CD6598562) b/w Heart And Soul (A Cappella Remix), Heart And Soul (Instrumental), A Dream Come True	75
06/12/1993	YOU'LL NEVER WALK ALONE with Barry Manilow (Columbia CD6600132) b/w You'll Never Walk Alone (Hope In Your Heart Mix), Through The Years	–
07/09/2009	SOMETHING TELLS ME: The Remixes (EMI/Digital Download) inc. Almighty Radio Edit, Original 1971 Single Mix, Dan Thomas Radio Edit & Arnold From Mumbai Remix	–
30/11/2009	STEP INSIDE LOVE: Tommy Sandhu Remixes (C.B. Ltd / Digital Download) inc. 2009 The Stunner Mix, 2002 Club Mix, 2002 Vacation Dub, 2002 Club Mix - Radio Edit & 2002 All Burnt Out Mix	–

SPECIALLY RECORDED INTERNATIONAL SINGLES

Release Date	A side b/w B side, Record Label & Catalogue Number	Highest Chart Pos.
1968	M'INNAMORO "Step Inside Love" (Dischi Ricordi S.P.A, Italy SIR20.080) b/w Non C'e Domani "Where Is Tomorrow?"	–
1969	QUANDO SI SPEZZA UN GRANDE AMORE "Surround Yourself With Sorrow" (Dischi Ricordi S.P.A, Italy SIR20.098) b/w Without Him	–
1976	FANTASY (Private Stock, USA PS45.077) b/w It's Now * The single was a 'Top 20' hit on Billboard's 'Dance Music/Club Play Singles' chart.	15*

U.K. EXTENDED PLAYS

Release Date	Title, Record Label, Catalogue & Tracks	Highest Chart Pos.
04/1964	ANYONE WHO HAD A HEART (Parlophone GEP8901) b/w Just For You, Love Of The Loved, Shy Of Love	5
10/1964	IT'S FOR YOU (Parlophone GEP8916) b/w He Won't Ask Me, You're My World, Suffer Now I Must	12
08/1966	CILLA'S HITS (Parlophone GEP8954) inc. Don't Answer Me, The Right One Is Left, Alfie, Night Time Is Here	6
06/1967	TIME FOR CILLA (Parlophone GEP8967) inc. Abyssinian Secret, Trees And Loneliness, There I Go, Time	–

STUDIO ALBUMS

Release Date	Title, Record Label, Catalogue & Tracks	Highest Chart Pos.
01/1965	CILLA (Parlophone PMC1243/PCS3063) Mono/Stereo) Goin' Out Of My Head, Every Little Bit Hurts, Baby It's You, Dancing In The Street, Come To Me, Ol' Man River, One Little Voice, I'm Not Alone Anymore, Whatcha Gonna Do 'Bout It, Love Letters, This Empty Place, You'd Be So Nice To Come Home To	5
04/1966	CILLA SINGS A RAINBOW (Parlophone PMC/PCS 7004) Mono/Stereo) Love's Just A Broken Heart, Lover's Concerto, Make It Easy On Yourself, One Two Three, (There's) No Place To Hide, When I Fall In Love, Yesterday, Sing A Rainbow, Baby I'm Yours, The Real Thing, Everything I Touch Turns To Tears, In A Woman's Eyes, My Love Come Home	4
04/1968	SHER-OO! (Parlophone PMC/PCS 7041) Mono/Stereo) What The World Needs Now Is Love, Suddenly You Love Me, This Is The First Time, Follow The Path Of The Stars, Misty Roses, Take Me In Your Arms And Love Me, Yo-Yo, Something's Gotten Hold Of My Heart, Step Inside Love, A Man And A Woman, I Couldn't Take My Eyes Off You, Follow Me	7
05/1969	SURROUND YOURSELF WITH CILLA (Parlophone PCS7079) Aquarius, Without Him, Only Forever Will Do, You'll Never Get To Heaven, Forget Him, It'll Never Happen Again, Think Of Me, I Am A Woman, Words, Red Rubber Ball, Liverpool Lullaby, Surround Yourself With Sorrow	–
07/1970	SWEET INSPIRATION (Parlophone PCS7103) Sweet Inspiration, Put A Little Love In Your Heart, The April Fools, I Can't Go On Living Without You, From Both Sides Now, Across The Universe, Black Paper Roses, Mysterious People, Dear Madame, Oh Pleasure Man, Little Pleasure Acre, For Once In My Life, Rule Britannia	42
05/1971	IMAGES (Parlophone PCS7128) Faded Images, Junk, Your Song, Just Friends, It's Different Now, First Of May, (They Long To Be) Close To You, Rainbow, Make It With You, Our Brand New World, Sad Sad Song, Bridge Over Troubled Water	–
01/1973	DAY BY DAY WITH CILLA (Parlophone PCS7155) Without You, Thank Heavens I've Got You, Help Me Jesus, The Long And Winding Road, I Hate Sunday, I Don't Know How To Love Him, Day By Day, I've Still Got My Heart Joe, Sleep Song, Gypsies Tramps And Thieves, Winterwood, Oh My Love	–
06/1974	IN MY LIFE (EMI 3031) Flashback, I'll Have To Say I Love You In A Song, Everything I Own, Baby We Can't Go Wrong, Someone, Daydreamer, In My Life, Never Run Out (Of You), Let Him In, The Air That I Breathe, Like A Song, I Believed It All	–
03/1976	IT MAKES ME FEEL GOOD (EMI 3108) Something About You, I'll Take A Tango, September Love Affair, Lay The Music Down, San Diego Serenade, Heartbeat, Running Out Of World, To Know Him Is To Love Him, It Makes Me Feel Good, Lay It All Down, One Step From Your Arms, Lovin' Land	–

06/1978 MODERN PRISCILLA (EMI 3232) –
Silly Boy, The Other Woman, Me And The Elephant, Keep Your Mind On Love,
Putting It Down To The Way I Feel, Sugar Daddy, Opening Night,
Brooklyn, I Couldn't Make My Mind Up, Heart Get Ready For Love,
Love Lines, Platform Rocker

08/1980 ESPECIALLY FOR YOU (K-TEL ONE1085) –
Baby Don't Change Your Mind, Sometimes When We Touch,
Just the Way You Are, Talking In Your Sleep, You Don't Bring Me
Flowers, How Deep Is Your Love, Bright Eyes, Don't Cry For Me
Argentina,When Will I See You Again, You Needed Me, If You Leave
Me Now, When I Need You, Knowing Me Knowing You, Still,
When A Child Is Born, Do That To Me One More Time

10/1985 SURPRISINGLY CILLA (Towerbell TOWLP14) –
Surprise Surprise, I Know Him So Well, You're My World (1985
Re-recording), One More Night, There's A Need In Me, Conversations
(1985 Re-recording), Step Inside Love (1985 Re-recording),
We're In This Love Together, I See Forever In Your Eyes, Put Your Heart
Where Your Love Is, That's Already Taken, You've Lost That
Lovin' Feelin' (1985 Re-recording)

11/1990 CILLA'S WORLD (Virgin, Australia CICHCD1) –
The (Solar Powered, Practical, Combustible, Compactable,
Responsibly, Recyclable) Machine, Don't Argue With An Elephant,
A Little More Green, ABC Of The World, Penguin Strut, Rain, Trees,
Eggs, Panda, Personality, Weather Song/Sunshine Medley,
Please Don't Call Me A Koala Bear, Let's Hear It For Skin,
The End Of The Day, Goodnight

09/1993 THROUGH THE YEARS (Columbia 4746502) 41
Through The Years, That's What Friends Are For (with Cliff Richard),
Here, There And Everywhere, Heart And Soul (with Dusty Springfield),
Anyone Who Had A Heart (1993 Re-recording), A Dream Come True,
You'll Never Walk Alone (with Barry Manilow), Streets Of London,
You're My World (1993 Re-recording), From A Distance,
Will You Love Me Tomorrow?, Through The Years (Reprise)

09/2003 BEGINNINGS (Greatest Hits & New Songs) (EMI 5931812) 68
Featuring these Newly Recorded songs: Kiss You All Over,
If You Could Read My Mind, Beginnings, Beautiful Goodbye,
Imagine (Backing Vocals by Cliff Richard), Let There Be Love,
This Kiss, My Man (You've Changed My Tune), Photograph,
I've Been Wrong Before, Anyone Who Had A Heart (Late Night Version),
Plus the album includes hidden track: Step Inside Love (All Burnt Out Mix)

CLUB REMIXES ALBUM

Release Date	Title, Record Label & Tracks	Highest Chart Pos.

09/2009 CILLA ALL MIXED UP (EMI/Digital Download) –
Featuring specially commissioned remixes of various 'classic' recordings:-
Step Inside Love (Almighty Radio Edit), Something Tells Me (Almighty Mix),
Anyone Who Had A Heart (Almighty Mix), Baby We Can't Go Wrong
(Almighty Radio Edit), I Don't Know How To Love Him (David Lee Marks
Radio Edit), Beautiful Goodbye (Klubkidz Extended Mix), Faded Images
(Tommy Sandhu's Ram Mix), Kiss You All Over (Tommy Sandhu's
Big Bill Mix), A Fool Am I (Marley M Remix), Your Song (Pookadelic Remix),
Step Inside Love (DJ Ronstar - Step In Da Club Mix), Something Tells Me
(Dan Thomas Club Mix)

SOUNDTRACK ALBUMS

Release Date	Title, Record Label & Tracks	Highest Chart Pos.

02/1965 FERRY ACROSS THE MERSEY (Columbia/EMI SCX3544) 19
"Is It Love?" the song Cilla performed in the movie appears on the soundtrack.

NOTABLE U.K. RE-ISSUE / COMPILATION ALBUMS

All CD Re-issues listed below contain 'Digitally Re-mastered' recordings: Highest Chart Pos.

Release Date	Title, Record Label & Catalogue	

12/1968 THE BEST OF CILLA BLACK (Parlophone PMC/PCS 7065) (Mono/Stereo) 21

01/1983 THE VERY BEST OF CILLA BLACK (Parlophone/EMI EMTV38) 20

05/1987 LOVE SONGS (K-TEL ONCD5126) –
First CD re-issue of Cilla's 1980 "Especially For You" album,
with different sleeve.

1991 THE BEST OF THE EMI YEARS (EMI CDEMS1410) –
First "Greatest Hits" compilation to be released in the U.K. on CD format.

09/1997 THE ABBEY ROAD DECADE 1963-73 (EMI CILLA1) –
A 3CD set containing Cilla's complete single A&B sides and her E.P.
recordings released by Parlophone Records. Plus a CD dedicated
to her very first recordings, rarities and previously unreleased tracks.

04/2002 CILLA/CILLA SINGS A RAINBOW (EMI 5388482) –
Mono CD issue of Cilla's 1965/66 studio albums.

08/2002 THE BEST OF CILLA BLACK (EMI 5414442) –
CD issue of Cilla's 1968 compilation. Includes 11
bonus singles and rarities.

05/2003 THE BEST OF 1963-78 (EMI 5841242) –
A 3-CD set containing 80 tracks recorded over 15 years. It features
essential recordings from album and single releases plus 7 previously
unreleased recordings and a comprehensive photo booklet with many
celebrity anecdotes. British music magazine 'Record Collector' selected
this set as a "New Release Highlight" of the entire year!

09/2005 CILLA IN THE 1960S (EMI 3369892) –
A 25-track, budget compilation CD featuring recording highlights
from the 1960s. Unearthed for this release was a rare Italian language
version of Cilla's hit song "Surround Yourself with Sorrow"
(aka "Quando Si Spezza Un Grande Amore").

09/2005 CILLA IN THE 1970S (EMI 3373132) –
A 24-track, budget compilation CD featuring recording highlights
from the 1970s. It includes an unreleased 1976 recording
"A Bad Case Of Rock 'N' Roll" (produced by David Mackay)
plus two alternate takes.

09/2009 THE DEFINITIVE COLLECTION (A Life In Music) (EMI 5099996723326) –
A career-spanning compilation containing 50 Parlophone/EMI recordings
on 2CDs - this includes all of Cilla's Top 40 U.K. hit singles, alternate
takes/versions and newly commissioned club remixes. It also
significantly features Cilla's first-ever music DVD of rare performances
which were filmed at the BBC between 1964 and 1976.

09/2009 The following Studio Albums were re-issued worldwide on –
Digital Download with informative digital booklets and
various bonus tracks/rarities:-

CILLA (EMI/Digital Download)
CILLA SINGS A RAINBOW (EMI/Digital Download)
SHER-OO! (EMI/Digital Download)
BEST OF CILLA: Mono Edition (EMI/Digital Download)
SURROUND YOURSELF WITH CILLA (EMI/Digital Download)
SWEET INSPIRATION (EMI/Digital Download)
IMAGES (EMI/Digital Download)
DAY BY DAY WITH CILLA (EMI/Digital Download)
IN MY LIFE (EMI/Digital Download)
IT MAKES ME FEEL GOOD (EMI/Digital Download)
MODERN PRISCILLA (EMI/Digital Download)
ESSENTIAL LOVE SONGS: ESPECIALLY FOR YOU
(C.B. Ltd /Digital Download)
BEGINNINGS: REVISITED (EMI/Digital Download)

04/2012 COMPLETELY CILLA: 1963-1973 (EMI 5099960283221) –
A multiple disc compilation of Cilla Black's "COMPLETE"
recordings with music producer George Martin. It contains
139 recordings on 5 CDs as well as a bonus DVD of previously
unavailable material from BBC TV's film archive.
Completely Cilla is the first compilation to present her
recordings in original session date order. An extensive
booklet is contained featuring new interviews with Cilla and
other key people who she worked with during her recording
career. Highlights on the DVD include stunning duets with
Cliff Richard ("Passing Strangers") and Hank Marvin,
Bruce Welch and John Farrar ("Norwegian Wood").

2013 THE 50TH ANNIVERSARY COLLECTION (PARLOPHONE #T.B.A.) –
The career-spanning compilation is released to celebrate Cilla's
50th year in showbusiness. The CD features Cilla's biggest and best-
loved chart hits from around the world alongside 2 newly
commissioned club remixes and her complete Parlophone/EMI
songbooks by John Lennon & Paul McCartney. A bonus DVD features
'CILLA AT THE SAVOY' - this top-rated 1966 TV special was recorded
live during a sell-out cabaret season at London's Savoy Hotel.

BACK
TO
BLACK

Evans Mitchell Books

With thanks to: Paul Mellor,
Tracey Fairweather and Dave Young

Picture Credits: Nicky Johnston, Getty Images,
Rex Features, The Cilla Black Archive (thanks to
Stephen Munns) and Parlophone Records.
While every effort has been made to contact
the copyright holders, we apologise for any
omissions and will be happy to include them
in any following editions of this publication.